The Oratorio Anthology

Tenor

Compiled and Edited by Richard Walters

Assistant Editors: Elaine Schmidt, Laura Ward
Repertoire Consultants: Kenneth Bozeman, Steven Stolen
Historical Consultant: Virginia Saya

On the cover: André Derain, French, *The Last Supper*, oil on canvas, 1911, 226.7 x 288.3 cm,
Gift of Mrs. Frank R. Lillie, 1946.339. © 1993, The Art Institute of Chicago, All Rights Reserved.

ISBN 0-7935-2507-1

HAL•LEONARD
CORPORATION
7777 W. BLUEMOUND RD. P.O. BOX 13819 MILWAUKEE, WI 53213

Contents

Notes and Translations

Carl Philipp Emanuel Bach
1714-1788

MAGNIFICAT
1750

text taken from Luke 1:46-55, from the Vulgate (the 4th century, authorized Roman Catholic Latin translation of the Bible); besides these verses a Magnificat (the canticle of the Virgin) traditionally includes two additional verses of the Lesser Doxology "Gloria Patri et Filio"

Composed 1749. Possibly first performed 1750, at Thomaskirche, Leipzig. The trumpet, timpani, and horn parts were added later to the original scoring.

Quia fecit mihi magna

Quia fecit mihi magna	*For he to me is mighty*
qui potens est:	*who has done great things:*
et sanctum nomen ejus.	*and holy is his name.*

Johann Sebastian Bach
1685-1750

MAGNIFICAT
BWV 243a and 243
1723

text taken from Luke 1:46-55, from the Vulgate (the 4th century, authorized Roman Catholic Latin translation of the Bible); besides these verses a Magnificat (the canticle of the Virgin) traditionally includes two additional verses of the Lesser Doxology "Gloria Patri et Filio"

Composed for Bach's first Christmas in Leipzig. It was later revised (c1728-1731) and transposed from E-flat to D. The revision replaces recorders with flutes and omits 4 interpolated hymns (laudes), which had previously rendered the text appropriate to the Christmas season. The revised Magnificat was possibly first performed July 2, 1733 for the Feast of the Visitation of Mary. The Magnificat was sung in German for Sunday vespers, and in Latin on Christmas Day.

Deposuit potentes

Scored for violins I and II in unison and continuo.

Deposuit potentes de sede	*He sets down the mighty from their seats*
et exaltavit humiles.	*and exalts the humble.*

Dates throughout are for first performances unless otherwise noted. The bracketed aria titles are those used when performing the singing English translation found in the musical score. The notes in this section are by the editor.

MASS IN B MINOR

composed 1724-1740s
text is the traditional Latin Mass from the Roman Catholic liturgy

Not initially conceived as a unity, the different sections of what would eventually be the Mass in B minor were composed over a period of perhaps as much as 25 years. The Sanctus was composed in 1724 and first performed on Christmas Day in that year at Thomaskirche, Leipzig. The Kyrie and Gloria sections, comprising what was then known as the Missa in Lutheran terminology, were composed and first performed in 1733, probably in Dresden. At some later point Bach composed the remaining sections with the result of a complete traditional mass. The sources are unclear, and there is disagreement about the dates of composition for the Credo, Osanna, Benedictus, Agnus Dei, and Dona nobis pacem. Among the new composition there was some significant borrowing of music from earlier works. Bach's work to complete the mass was probably done in the 1740s, with theories that put it as late as 1748 or 1749, which would make the Mass in B minor perhaps the composer's last major composition. (*The Art of the Fugue* was probably principally composed early in the decade.) Earlier historical theories stated that these remaining sections were composed at different times, primarily in the 1730s, and that Bach assembled the mass into a whole near the end of his life. The first performance of the complete work was in 1859 in Leipzig.

Benedictus

Scored for flute and continuo.

Benedictus qui venit	*Blessed is he who comes*
in nomine Domini.	*in the name of the Lord.*

PASSIO SECUNDUM JOANNEM

(Johannes-Passion/St. John Passion)
BWV 245
1724
libretto based primarily on *Der für die Sünden der Welt gemarterte und sterbende Jesus* (Jesus tortured and dying for the sins of the world) by Barthold Heinrich Brockes (1712), with some additional free texts from a 1704 Passion libretto by Christian Heinrich Postel (free text refers to poetry that is not an adaptation or paraphrase of Scripture), with adaptations and additional material by the composer

Composed in 1723, the Passion was first performed on Good Friday, April 7, 1724 at Thomaskirche, Leipzig. The piece was revised, with additions, deletions and substitutions, for performances in 1725, but basically restored to the original version for performances in c1730 and 1740. A Passion is a musical setting of Jesus' sufferings and death as related by one of the four Gospel writers. Brockes' libretto, cited above, was the most often set of Passion librettos by composers in the 18th century.

Ach, mein Sinn

From Part I (no. 19), scored for strings (doubled by woodwinds, ad. lib.), bassoon, and continuo. This is a free text by Brockes. The words are Simon Peter's following his denial of Jesus. In the 1725 revision of the Passion, this aria was replaced with "Zerschmettert mich, ihr Felsen und ihr Hügel."

Ach, mein Sinn,	*Oh, my soul,*
wo willst du endlich hin,	*were will you finally go,*
wo soll ich mich erquikken?	*where shall I refresh myself?*
Bleib' ich hier,	*Remain I here*
oder wünsch' ich mir	*or desire I myself*
Berg und Hügel auf den Rükken?	*on the ridge of mountain and hill?*
Bei der Welt ist gar kein Rat,	*In the world is absolutely no counsel,*
und im Herzen stehn die Schmerzen	*and in the heart remains the pain*
meiner Missetat,	*of my crime,*
weil der Knecht	*because the servant*
den Herrn verleugnet hat.	*has denied the Lord.*

PASSIO SECUNDUM MATTHÆUM

(Matthäus-Passion/St. Matthew Passion)
BWV 244
1727 or 1729
libretto by Picander, a pseudonym for Christian Friedrich Henrici (1700-1764); it is probable that the free text poems only were by Henrici (free text refers to poetry that is not a paraphrase or adaptation directly from Scripture), with adapted biblical narrative from the Gospel of Matthew and some chorale texts by the composer

The date of first performance of the Passion is in dispute, occuring at Thomaskirche, Leipzig, on either April 11, 1727 or April 15, 1729. A revised version was performed March 30, 1736. A Passion is a musical setting of Jesus' sufferings and death as related by one of the four Gospel writers.

Geduld, Geduld   *[Be still, be still]*

From Part II (nos. 40, 41). The recitative is scored for oboes and continuo; the aria is scored for continuo. The recitative describes Jesus' silent reaction to the interview with the high priest. The aria is composed to a free text.

Mein Jesus schweigt	*My Jesus is silent*
zu falschen Lügen stille,	*to false-lies still,*
um uns damit zu zeigen,	*around us therewith to show,*
dass sein erbarmensvoller Wille	*that his compassionate will*
vor uns zum Leiden sei geneigt,	*for us is inclined to sorrow*
und dass wir in der gleichen Pein	*and that we in the same torment*
ihm sollen ähnlich sein,	*to him should similar be,*
und Verfolgung stille schweigen.	*and in persecution be silent.*
Geduld, Geduld!	*Patience, patience!*
wenn mich falsche Zungen stechen.	*when false tongues stab me.*
Leid' ich wider meine Schuld	*Suffer I against my guilt*
Schimpf und Spott,	*disgrace and scorn,*
leid ich Schimpf und Spott,	*suffer I disgrace and scorn,*
ei! so mag der liebe Gott	*indeed, so wants the loving God*
meines Herzens Unschuld rächen.	*my heart's innocence to avenge.*

WEIHNACHTS-ORATORIUM

(Christmas Oratorio)
BWV 248
1734-1735
text attributed to Picander, a pseudonym for Christian Friedrich Henrici (1700-1764); based on Luke 2:1, 3-12, and Matthew 1:1-12 (the Luther German Bible)

The Weihnachts-Oratorium is actually a collection of six individual church cantatas, designed to be performed at each of the six church events between Christmas and Epiphany. The piece contains newly composed music, and adaptations from three secular cantatas (BWV 213-215). The first cantata was first performed on Christmas Day, 1734 at Thomaskirche, Leipzig. The remaining cantatas followed in order on the second and third days following Christmas, on New Year's Day (Feast of the Circumcision), on the Sunday after New Year, and on the Feast of the Epiphany. Performances took place at both Thomaskirche and Nikolaikirche, Leipzig.

Frohe Hirten, eilt, ach eilet   *[Haste, ye shepherds]*

From Part II (the second cantata), Second Christmas Day, scored for flute (or flutes) and continuo.

Frohe Hirten,	*Joyful shepherds,*
eilt, ach eilet,	*hasten, oh hurry,*
eh ihr euch zu lang verweilet,	*before you too long remain,*
eilt, das holde Kind zu sehn!	*hurry, the sweet child to see!*
Geht, die Freude heisst zu schön,	*Go, the joy is too beautiful,*
sucht die Anmut zu gewinnen,	*seek the grace to gain,*
geht, und labet Herz und Sinnen.	*go, and refresh your heart and soul.*

Ludwig van Beethoven
1770-1827

CHRISTUS AM ÖLBERGE
(Christ on the Mount of Olives)
Opus 85
1803
libretto by Franz Xaver Huber, based on the Gospel accounts of Jesus in the Garden of Gethsemane

First performed April 5, 1803 at the Theater am Wien (Vienna). Revised 1804-1811. The aria is presented in the final form.

Meine Seele ist erschüttert

Jesus is praying in the Garden of Gethsemane.

Jehova, du mein Vater!	*Jehovah, you, my Father!*
o sende Trost und Kraft und Stärke mir.	*O send comfort and strength and power to me.*
Sie nahet nun, die Stunde meiner Leiden.	*It approaches now, the hour of my sorrow.*
Von mir erkoren schon, noch eh' die Welt	*By me chosen already, yet before the world*
auf dein Geheiss dem Chaos sich entwand.	*at your command the chaos burst forth.*
Ich höre deines Seraphs Donnerstimme,	*I hear your Seraph's thunderous voice*
sie fordert auf, wer statt der menschen sich	*they call out, who for the people*
vor dein Gericht jetzt stellen will.	*before your judgement now will stand.*
O Vater!	*O Father!*
ich erschein' auf diesen Ruf.	*I appear at this call.*
Vermittler will ich sein,	*Mediator will I be,*
ich büsse, ich allein,	*I atone, I alone,*
der Menschen Schuld.	*humanity's guilt.*
Wie könnte dies Geschlecht,	*How can this species,*
aus Staub gebildet	*out of dust formed*
ein Gericht ertragen,	*a judgement endure,*
das mich, mich, deinen Sohn,	*which me, me, your Son*
zu Boden drückt?	*to the grave pushes.*
Ach sieh! wie Bangigkeit,	*Oh see! How fearfulness*
wie Todesangst	*how mortal terror*
mein Herz mit Macht ergreift!	*my heart with might sieze!*
ich leide sehr, mein Vater!	*I suffer greatly my Father!*
sieh!	*Oh see!*
ich leide sehr,	*I suffer greatly,*
erbarm' dich mein!	*have mercy on me.*
Meine Seele ist erschüttert	*My soul trembles*
von den Qualen,	*from the torment,*
die mir dräun.	*that threatens me.*
Schrecken fasst mich,	*Terror grasps me,*
und es zittert grässlich	*and I shudder horribly*
schaudernd mein Gebein.	*my body shivers.*
Wie ein Fieberfrost	*As a fever-chill*
ergreifet mich die Angst	*siezes me the anguish*
im nahen Grab,	*of the nearby grave,*
und von meinem Antlitz träufet	*and from my face drips*
statt des Schweisses Blut herab.	*instead of the sweat, blood.*
Vater! tief gebeugt und kläglich	*Father! deeply bent and pitiful*
fleht dein Sohn hinauf zu dir:	*entreats your Son up to you:*
deiner Macht ist Alles möglich,	*in your power is all possible*
nimm den Leidenskelch von mir!	*take the cup of sorrow from me!*

Anton Bruckner
1824-1896

TE DEUM LAUDAMUS
1886
text is a traditional Latin hymn of praise, formerly attributed to St. Ambrose, but possibly written by the 6th century bishop Nicetus, with some lines taken from De mortalitate (A.D. 272) of St. Cyprian

Composed 1881-1884. First performed January 10, 1886, Vienna. The Te Deum is used in the Roman Catholic liturgy, often replacing the last responsory of Matins on feast days and Sundays, and in the Anglican church as one of the canticles of Morning Prayer. It is also sung as a hymn on various occasions, particularly as a thanksgiving.

Te ergo quæsumus

Te ergo quæsumus,	*You therefore I beg,*
tuis famulis subveni;	*Your servants relieve;*
quos pretioso sanguine redemisti	*who You with Your precious blood redeemed*
quos redemisti.	*who You redeemed.*

Charles Gounod
1818-1893

MESSE SOLENNELLE DE STE CÉCILE
(St. Cecilia Mass)
1855
text is the traditional Latin Mass from the Roman Catholic Liturgy

Sections of what would later become the St. Cecilia Mass, including the Sanctus, were first performed in London, January 5, 1851 in Gounod's British debut. The completed mass was first performed November 29, 1855 at the Church of Saint-Eustache, Paris. The Sanctus begins with a tenor solo, and then becomes largely a choral movement.

Sanctus

Sanctus Dominus;	*Holy Lord;*
Sanctus Deus Sabaoth.	*Holy God of the heavenly Hosts.*
Pleni sunt cœli et terra gloria tua.	*Heaven and earth are full of your glory.*

George Frideric Handel
1685-1759

ATHALIA
1733
libretto by Samuel Humphreys, adapted from Jean Racine's 1691 play *Athalie*; the story is based on II Kings 2

The oratorio was first performed July 10, 1733 at the Sheldonian Theatre, Oxford.

Gentle airs, melodious strains!

From Act I, Mathan, a Baalite priest, comforts Athalia after a nightmare.

[IS]RAEL IN EGYPT

[173]9

[Libr]etto is biblical, assembled from Exodus I:8, 11, 13, Exodus II:23, Psalm 105, Psalm 106, Exodus XV:1-21

[Firs]t performed April 4, 1739 at the King's Theatre, Haymarket, London.

[Th]e enemy said

[Fro]m Act III, based on Exodus 15:9.

[JE]PHTHA

[175]2

[Libr]etto by Thomas Morell (1703-1784), quoting and paraphrasing Judges 11, *Jephthes Sive Votum* (1554) by
[George] Buchanan, Milton's "Nativing Ode," Addison's "The Campaign," and John Pope's "Essay on Man"

[Firs]t performance at the Theatre Royal at Covent Garden, London, February 26, 1752. *Jephtha* was revived in 1758 "with new additions
[and] alterations." The oratorio is based on the story of the Jews' defeat of the Ammonites.

[Wa]ft her, angels

[Th]e recitative ("Hide thou thy hated beams") and aria open Act III, sung by Jephtha of Gilead, leader of the army of Israel. In prayer, he
[has] made a vow to sacrifice to God whoever comes through the doors of his house upon his return if the Lord gives him victory over the
[Am]monites. Victorious, Jephtha returns home, and Iphis, his daughter, is the first to appear. She nobly accepts her fate, though Jephtha's
[hea]rt is broken.

[JU]DAS MACCABÆUS

[174]7

[Libr]etto by Thomas Morell (1703-1784), based on the book of the Maccabees and the twelfth book of Josephus' *Antiquities of the Jews*

[Co]mmissioned by Frederic, Prince of Wales. First performed at the Theatre Royal at Covent Garden, London, April 1, 1747. Revisions
[and] additions were made for frequent new productions, in 1748, then annually from 1750, to 1759. The oratorio relates the restoration
[of li]berty to the Jews under leader Judas Maccabæus.

[Sou]nd an alarm!

[Fro]m Act II, Judas is calling the Israelites to armas after the news of an advancing Syrian army.

[M]ESSIAH

[174]2

[Text] by Charles Jennens (1700-1773), drawn from various biblical sources and the Prayer Book Psalter

[Co]mposed between August 22 and September 12, 1741. First performed April 13, 1742 at the Music Hall on Fishamble Street, Dublin.
[Th]e performance was a benefit for several of the city's charities. The libretto is drawn from the Prophets, the Gospels, the Pauline Epistles,
[and] Revelation, detailing the prophecy of Christ's coming, his life, death, resurrection, promise of second coming, and the response of
[belie]vers. *Messiah* is theological in nature, not the more common dramatic Handelian oratorio. The soloists are impersonal, and the cho-
[rus] assumes an expanded role as commentators. Many changes and additions were made in the oratorio, with 13 revisions of the score in
[the] years 1743-1759. Many of the solo movements were sometimes sung by different voice types in different versions and keys, a practice
[the] composer directed.

[Co]mfort ye, my people; Ev'ry valley shall be exalted

[Fro]m Part I. The text is based on Isaiah 40:1-3.

[Be]hold, and see if there be any sorrow; But Thou didst not leave His soul in hell

[Fro]m Part II. The recitative "Thy rebuke hath broken his heart" is based on Psalm 69:20. "Behold, and see if there be any sorrow" is based
[on] Lamentations 1:12. The recitative "He was cut off" is from Isaiah 53:8. "But Thou didst not leave His soul in hell" is from Psalm
[16:]10. This section, originally intended for tenor solo, was during Handel's time variously assigned to tenor and soprano soloists.

Thou shalt break them

From Part II. The recitative that precedes the aria is based on Psalm 11:4. The aria is based on Psalm 11:9. Handel also set the text as a recitative, apparently for a tenor who was not up to the vocal demands of the aria.

SAMSON
1743
libretto adapted by Newburgh Hamilton from Milton's *Samson Agonistes* and other poems

Composed 1741. First performed February 18, 1743, at the Theatre Royal at Covent Garden, London. Additions and revisions were made for performances in 1745 and 1754. The oratorio relates the story from Judges, with the addition of the character of Micah.

Total eclipse

From Act I. Samson mourns his blindness.

Franz Joseph Haydn
1732-1809

DIE JAHRESZEITEN
(The Seasons)
1801
libretto by Baron Gottfried van Swieten after "The Seasons," a lengthy pastoral poem by James Thomson, translated into German by Barthold Heinrich Brockes

Begun in 1799, the oratorio was first performed May 20, 1801. Under Haydn's direction and consent, a singing English translation by Swieten (adapting the original poem by Thomson) was included in the first edition of the oratorio, published in 1802 by Breikopf & Härtel. (A German-French edition was also released at the same time.) The aria below is from Winter.

Hier steht der Wand'rer nun	*[The trav'ler stands perplexed]*
Gefesselt steht der breite See,	*Chained stands the wide sea*
gehemmt in seinem Laufe der Strom.	*arrested is the current of the river.*
Im Sturtze vom türmenden	*In the tumble of piled-up*
Felsen hängt,	*rocks hangs,*
gestockt und stumm der Wasserfall.	*dry and silent the waterfall.*
Im dürren Haine tönt kein Laut.	*In the barren wood rings no sound.*
Die Felder deckt,	*The field is covered,*
die Täler füllt	*the valley is full*
ein' ungeheure Flokkenlast.	*of an enormous weight of snow.*
Der Erde Bild	*The earth picture*
ist nun ein Grab,	*is but a grave,*
wo Kraft und Reiz erstorben liegt,	*where strength and splendor lie,*
wo Leichenfarbe trauig herrscht,	*where pallor of mournful death prevails,*
und wo dem Blicke weit unher	*and where the glance wide about*
nur öde Wüstenei sich zeigt.	*only desolate desert reveals.*
Hier steht der Wand'rer nun	*Here stands the wanderer now*
verwirrt und zweifelhaft,	*confused and doubtful*
wohin den Schritt er lenken soll.	*where his step he should turn.*
Vergebens suchet er den Weg,	*In vain he seeks the way,*
ihn leitet weder Pfad noch Spur.	*he is led by neither path nor trail.*
Vergebens strenget er sich an,	*In vain he pushes himself on,*
und watet durch den tiefen Schnee,	*and wades through the deep snow,*
er find't sich immer mehr verirrt.	*he finds himself ever more confused.*
Jetzt sinket ihm der Mut,	*Now he sinks his courage*
und Angst beklemmt sein Herz,	*and fear oppresses his heart*
da er den Tag sich neigen sieht,	*that he sees the day of his decline*
und Müdigkeit und Frost	*and weariness and chill*

ihm alle Glieder lähmt.	*makes all his limbs lame.*
Jetzt sinket ihm der Mut,	*Now sinks his courage*
und Angst beklemmt sein Herz:	*and fear oppresses his heart:*
doch plötzlich trifft sein spähend Aug'	*but suddenly meets his eye*
der Schimmer eines nahen Lichts.	*the glimmer of approaching light.*
Da lebt er wieder auf,	*Then lives he again*
vor Freuden pocht sein Herz.	*with joy beats his heart.*
Er geht, er eilt der Hütte zu,	*He goes, he hastens to the cabin*
wo starr und matt er Labung hofft.	*where stiff and feeble he hopes for refreshment.*

DIE SCHÖPFUNG
Ein Oratorium für jeden Geschmack und jede Zeit
THE CREATION
An Oratorio for All Tastes and Times
1798

Libretto attributed to T. Linley or Lidley (sources are unclear about his name), translated from the original English to German and abridged by Baron Gottfried van Swieten, based on chapters from Genesis, selected Psalms, and paraphrases of Milton's *Paradise Lost*

Composition began in 1796. A first, private performance of the oratorio was given April 30, 1798 at the Schwartzenberg Palais (preceded by an open rehearsal April 29). The first public performance was given March 19, 1799. Haydn composed the piece in German, but the English version followed quickly, being basically the original libretto adapted by Swieten. (One of the primary manuscript scores used by Haydn to conduct has both German and English.) English was included in the first published edition, 1800. Since it was the composer's intention that the piece be heard in English in English-speaking countries, in the editor's opinion that is the appropriate language in those locales.

In 1801 Haydn composed a Mass in B-flat that is known as *Schöpfungmesse* (Creation Mass), but this piece is entirely different from the oratorio *Die Schöpfung*. (In the "qui tollis" of the mass Haydn quotes from the oratorio *Die Schöpfung*.)

Mit Würd' und Hoheit angetan

[In native worth]

Und Gott schuf den Menschen	*And God created the people*
nach seinem Ebenbilde.	*after his image.*
Nach dem Ebenbilde Gottes schuf er ihn.	*After the image of God he created them.*
Mann und Weib erschuf er sie.	*Man and wife he created them.*
Den Atem des Lebens hauchte	*Then the breath of life breathed*
in sein Angesicht	*into his face*
und der Mensch wurde zur lebendigen Seele.	*and the man became a living soul.*
Mit Würd und Hoheit angetan,	*With majesty and grandeur clad,*
mit Schönheit, Stark' und Mut begabt,	*with beauty, strength and boldness endowed,*
gen Himmel aufgerichtet steht der Mensch,	*heavenwards erect stands the human,*
ein Mann und König der Natur.	*a man and king of nature.*
Die breit gewölbt', erhab'ne Stirn,	*The broad arching, noble brow,*
verkünd't der Weisheit tiefen Sinn,	*proclaims the mind's deep wisdom,*
und aus dem hellen Blikke strahlt der Geist,	*and from the bright gaze radiates the spirit,*
des Schöpfers Hauch und Ebenbild.	*of the Creator's breath and image.*
An seinen Busen schmieget sich, für ihn,	*Against his breast nesltes, for him,*
aus ihm geformt,	*after him formed,*
die Gattin hold und anmutsvoll.	*the wife lovely and charming.*
In froher Unschuld lächelt sie,	*In glad innocence she smiles,*
des Frühlings reizend Bild,	*a charming picture of spring,*
ihm Liebe, Glück und Wonne zu.	*his beloved, happiness and joy.*

STABAT MATER

1767

text is traditional Latin from the Roman Catholic liturgy, a 13th century sequence attributed to the Franciscan Jacopone da Todi

Composed 1767, Eszterháza. No record of a performance exists from around that time, but the work was performed in the 1770s at Piaristenkirche in Vienna, conducted by the composer. Stabat Mater (literally translated as "mother standing") refers to Mary standing at the base of the cross. This text is still used in the Roman Catholic Church for the Feast of the Seven Sorrows (September 15).

Fac me cruce custodiri

Fac me cruce custodiri,	*May I by the cross be guarded*
morte Christi præmuniri,	*by the death of Christ fortified,*
Conservari gratia.	*sustained by Thy grace.*

Felix Mendelssohn

1809-1847

ELIJAH

(Elias)
Opus 70
1846

libretto by Julius Schubring, after I Kings 17-19, II Kings 2, and other biblical passages; English libretto by William Bartholomew

Composed summer of 1846. First performed August 26, 1846, the Birmingham Festival, England. William Bartholomew was given the *Elijah* libretto in the middle of May, 1846, and was engaged to translate it into English for the August premiere, receiving sections as they were completed. Mendelssohn and Schubring had used Luther's translation of the Bible, interpolating and paraphrasing liberally. Bartholomew's task was not only to translate, but also to make the text agree with the King James Bible. He added the following disclaimer to the libretto of *Elijah:* "The author of this English version has endeavored to render it as nearly in accordance with the Scriptural Texts as the Music to which it is adapted will admit: the references are therefore to be considered rather as authorities than quotations."

The arias are presented in both English, the language of the premiere, and German, the working language of Mendelssohn's composition. It may be assumed that the composer intended for English speaking audiences to hear the piece in the vernacular.

If with all your hearts (So ihr mich von ganzen Herzen suchet)

The tenor role of Obadiah has this aria in Act I, preaching to the people.

Then shall the righteous shine forth (Dann werden die Gerechten leuchten)

The aria, from Act II, comes just after Elijah has gone "by a whirlwind to heaven."

LOBGESANG

(Hymn of Praise)
1840
Text compiled from various Biblical passages

Composed for the Gutenberg Festival in Leipzig, commemorating the invention of printing, and first performed there at the Thomaskirche in 1840. Within a year the piece was performed in English at the Birmingham Festival in England, with Mendelssohn conducting. The Scriptural sources for the aria are adapted from Psalm 116 and Ephesians 5:14.

Strikke des Todes

[The Sorrows of Death]

Strikke des Todes	Ropes of death
hatten uns umfangen,	had us tied up
und Angst der Hölle	and fear of hell
hatte uns getroffen,	had hit us;
wir wandelten in Finsternis.	we wandered in darkness.
Er aber spricht: Wache auf!	He but speaks: Awake!
der du schläfst,	you who sleep,
stehe auf von den Toten,	stand up before death,
ich will dich erleuchten!	I will illuminate you.

PAULUS
(St. Paul)
1836
Libretto by J. Schubring, after the Acts of the Apostles

Composition began in 1834. The oratorio was originally commissioned for the St. Cecilia Society in Frankfurt, but because of the presenter's illness, the premiere was instead given at the Düsseldorf Festival (for which Mendelssohn was a director) on May 22, 1836. The piece was heavily revised for the first published edition (1837, Novello), which contained German and English. The revised *Paulus* was performed in March of 1837 in Frankfurt.

Sei getreu bis in den Tod

[Be thou faithful unto death]

Sei getreu bis in den Tod,	Be you faithful unto death,
will ich dir die Krone	so will I you the crown
des Lebens geben.	of life give.
Fürchte dich nicht,	Fear not,
ich bin bei dir,	I am with you,
fürchte dich nicht!	fear not! fear not!

Giacomo Puccini
1858-1924

MESSA DI GLORIA
1880
Text is the traditional Latin Mass from the Roman Catholic liturgy

Composed in 1880 as Puccini's final exam at the conservatory at Lucca. The mass also contains a Mottetto and a Credo that date from 1878. First performed July 12, 1880, Lucca, on the feast-day of St. Paulino (the patron saint of bells).

Gratias agimus tibi

Gratias agimus tibi	We give you thanks
propter magnam gloriam tuam.	for your great glory.

Gioachino Rossini
1792-1868

MESSE SOLENNELLE
1864
text is the traditional Latin Mass from the Roman Catholic liturgy

Composed in 1863, first performed in Paris, March 14, 1864, at the dedication of the private chapel of Countess Louise Pillet-Will. This original version was for 4 soloists, a chorus of 8 voices, 2 pianos and harmonium. The piece is often called "Petite Messe Solennelle," referring to the chamber music scale of the design, not because of brevity or liturgical reasons. Revised in 1867 for full orchestra. This second version was performed in Paris at the Théâtre-Italien, February 24, 1869.

Domine Deus

Domine Deus rex cœlestis	*Lord God, heavenly king*
Deus Pater omnipotens	*God the Father almighty*
Domine fili unigenite	*the only begotten Son*
Jesu Christe	*Jesus Christ*
Domine Deus	*Lord God*
Agnus Dei	*Lamb of God*
Filius Patris.	*Son of the Father.*

STABAT MATER
1832; 1842
text is traditional Latin from the Roman Catholic liturgy, a 13th century sequence attributed to the Franciscan Jacopone da Todi

First performed on Good Friday, 1833 at Cappella di San Filippo El Real, Madrid. Due to illness, Rossini requested that Giovanni Tadolini compose six of the twelve sections in order to complete the work for the premiere. In 1841 Rossini replaced the six Tadolini movements with new composition. The revised Stabat Mater was first performed January 7, 1842 at the Théâtre Italien, Paris. Stabat Mater (literally translated as "mother standing") refers to Mary standing at the base of the cross. The text of the Stabat Mater is still used the Roman Catholic Church for the Feast of the Seven Sorrows (September 15).

Cujus animam gementem

Cujus animam gementem,	*Whose soul laments*
contristantem et dolentem,	*sorrowful and anguished,*
pertransivit gladius.	*pierced by a sword.*
O quam tristis et afflicta	*Oh how sad and in pain*
fuit illa benedicta	*is she that was blessed*
Mater unigeniti;	*mother of the only begotten*
Quæ mœrebat, et dolebat et tremebat,	*who mourns, and suffers pain and trembles*
cum videbat nati pœnas inclyti.	*for her child bent in punishment.*

Camille Saint-Saëns
1835-1921

ORATORIO DE NOËL
(Christmas Oratorio)
Opus 12
1858
text is Latin, 9 parts from versicles of the Office of the Day and Midnight

Composed in 12 days in December, 1858. First performed Christmas Day, 1858, Paris. Scored for strings, harp, and organ. A versicle, Roman Catholic and Anglican services, is a short scriptural text sung by the leader, with the choir or congregation responding.

Domine, ego credidi

Domine, ego credidi,	*Lord, I trust,*
quia tu es Christus	*that you are Christ*
Filius Dei vivi,	*Son of God incarnate,*
qui in hunc mundum venisti.	*who came into this world.*

Giuseppe Verdi
1813-1901

MESSA DI REQUIEM
1874
text is the traditional Latin Requiem Mass from the Roman Catholic liturgy; Requiem ("rest") is a mass for the dead

The piece has a long history of development. In November, 1868, Verdi sent his publisher, Ricordi, a letter proposing a Requiem Mass, written by Italian composers, to honor Rossini, who had died early in the month. There was to be one performance only, on the first anniversary of Rossini's death, and no one was to profit from the work. Verdi was assigned the "Libera me" section of the mass, and completed composition in August. Severe conflicts and controversies prevented the "Rossini Requiem" from being presented. (It wasn't heard until 1988 at the Parma Cathedral.) In 1873 the Italian novelist Alessandro Manzoni died. Verdi proposed to Ricordi that he would write a Requiem in honor of Manzoni, and like the "Rossini Requiem," wanted to have the first performance on the first anniversary of Manzoni's death. Verdi incorporated the "Libera me" section that he had composed five years earlier. The Messa di Requiem was first performed May 22, 1874 at the Church of San Marco, Milan.

Ingemisco

Ingemisco tamquam reus:	*Groaning in shame,*
Culpa rubet vultus meus:	*Guilt reddening my face,*
Supplicanti parce Deus.	*Kneeling small before God.*
Qui Mariam absolvisti,	*Who released Mary,*
Et latronem exaudisti,	*And forgave the dying thief,*
Mihi quoque spem dedisti,	*I also surrender hope,*
Preces meæ non sunt dignæ,	*My prayers are not worthy,*
Sed tu bonus fac benigne,	*Without your divine kindness allowing,*
Ne perenni cremer igne.	*What could save me from undying fires.*
Inter oves locum præsta,	*With thy favored sheep place me,*
Et ab hædis me sequestra,	*And place me away from goats,*
Statuens in parte dextra.	*Standing with those at thy right hand.*

Antonio Vivaldi
1678-1741

BEATUS VIR
RV597
text is Psalm 111 from the Vulgate (the 4th century, authorized Roman Catholic Latin translation of the Bible), which is Psalm 112 in the Protestant Bible

No clear chronology exists for Vivaldi's sacred works. Note that this Beatus Vir in C is a completely different piece from Vivaldi's Beatus Vir in B-flat, RV 598.

Peccator videbit

Peccator videbit	*The wicked will see*
irascetur,	*and be angry,*
dentibus suis	*gnash their teeth*
fremet ettabescet:	*and pine away:*
desiderium peccatorum peribit.	*the desire of the wicked will perish.*

Quia fecit mihi magna
from
MAGNIFICAT

Carl Philipp Emanuel Bach

(lower octave is optional)

et sanc - tum no - men e - jus.

Deposuit potentes
from
MAGNIFICAT

Johann Sebastian Bach

28

vit hu – mi – les.

Benedictus
from
MASS IN B MINOR

Johann Sebastian Bach

*Small size notes are to be played only in the absence of a violin solo.

di - ctus   qui - ve - nit in no - mi-ne Do - mi - ni.

Be - ne - di - ctus, be - ne - di - ctus ____ qui

-nit, qui ve - nit in no - mi-ne Do - mi - ni.

Benedictus
from
MASS IN B MINOR

Johann Sebastian Bach

The part may be carefully cut from the book.

Ach, mein Sinn

from
PASSIO SECUNDUM JOANNEM
(St. John Passion)

Johann Sebastian Bach

44

81

tat, ___ weil der Knecht ___ den Herrn ver-leug - - - net

85

hat, weil der Knecht den Herrn ver - leug -

88

- net ___ hat.

Geduld, Geduld
(Be still, be still)
from
PASSIO SECUNDUM MATTHÆUM
(St. Matthew Passion)

Johann Sebastian Bach

*appoggiatura possible

Aria

[Larghetto]

Ge - duld.   Ge - duld!
Be   still,   be   still!

Ge -
Be

27

chen, ___ ei! so mag der lie - be Gott mei-nes Her - zens ___ Un - schuld rä -
thee; ___ Wait, and trust thy Sav-ior's Name, His de-fense ___ will ___ nev - er fail ___

29

chen.
thee.

f

31

Leid' ___ ich,   leid' ___ ich,
Let ___ them,   let ___ them,

p

33

leid' ich __ wi - der mei - ne Schuld Schimpf und Spott, Schimpf und
let them __ seek __ to work thee ill, Bring thee shame, bring thee

35

Spott, ei! so mag der __ lie - be __ Gott mei-nes Her - zens __ Un - schuld rä -
shame, Wait, and trust thy __ Sav - ior's __ Name, His de-fense __ will __ nev - er fail _____

37

chen.
thee.

f

Frohe Hirten, eilt, ach eilet

(Haste, ye shepherds)

from

WEIHNACHTS-ORATORIUM

(Christmas Oratorio)

Johann Sebastian Bach

*Small size notes are to be played only in the absence of a flute.

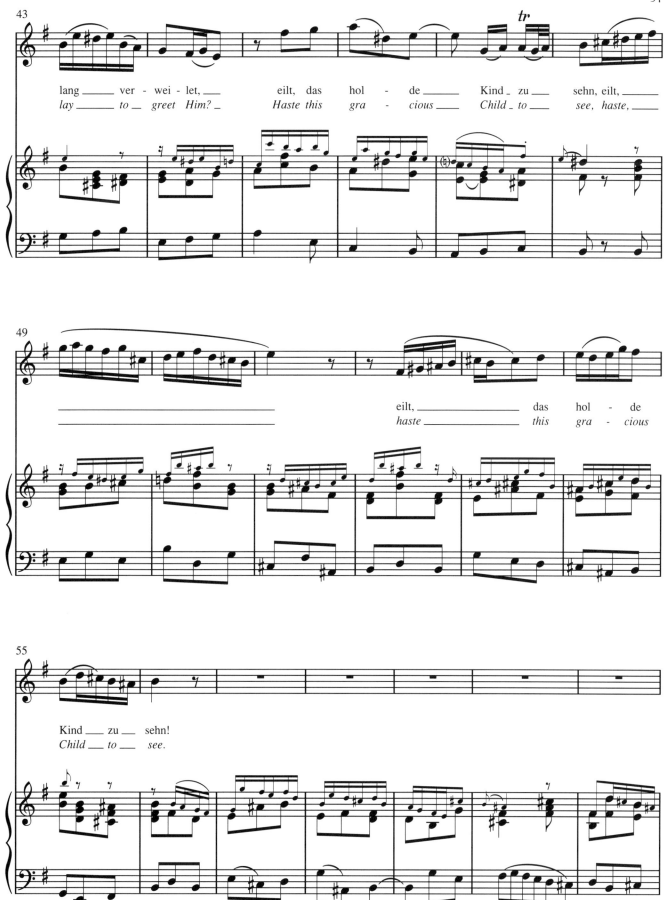

Geht, _ die Freu - - de heisst zu schön,
Glad _ and joy - - ful ye should be,

geht, __ die Freu - - de heisst zu schön, sucht __ die __
glad __ and joy - - ful ye should be, Of _____ His __

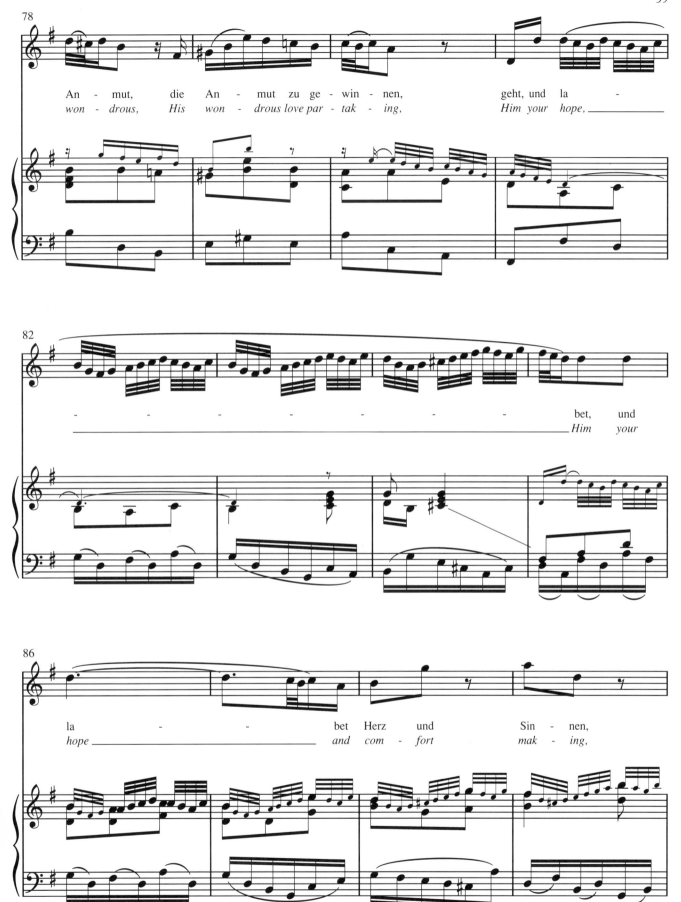

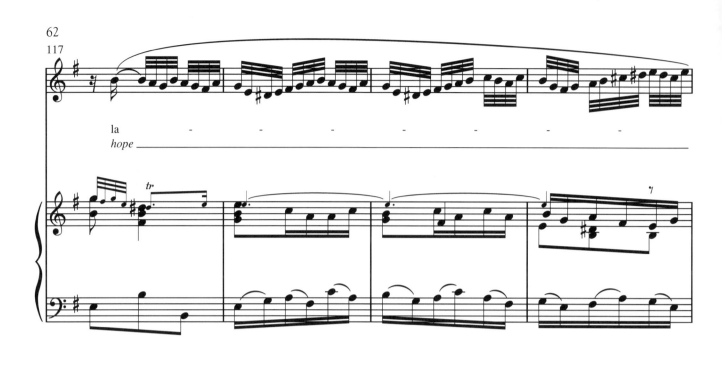

117

la - - - - - - -
hope _____

121

- - bet Herz _____ und Sin - nen.
_____ *and com - fort mak - ing.*

126

Frohe Hirten, eilt, ach eilet

(Haste, ye shepherds)

from

WEIHNACHTS-ORATORIUM

(Christmas Oratorio)

Johann Sebastian Bach

The part may be carefully cut from the book.

Meine Seele ist erschüttert

from
CHRISTUS AM ÖLBERGE
(Christ on the Mount of Olives)

Ludwig van Beethoven

Von mir er-ko-ren schon, noch eh' die Welt auf dein Ge - heiss dem Cha - os sich ent-

wand.

Ich hö - re dei-nes Ser-aphs Don-ner-stim-me, sie for-dert auf, wer statt der

Men-schen sich vor dein Ge-richt jetzt stel-len will.

O Va-ter! ich er-schein' auf die-sen Ruf. Ver-mitt-ler will ich

sein, ich büs-se, ich al - lein, der Men-schen Schuld. Wie könn-te dies Ge-

schlecht, aus Staub ge - bil-det ein Ge-richt er - tra-gen, das

mich, mich, dei-nen Sohn, _____ zu Bo-den drückt?

Adagio agitato

Ach sieh! _ wie Bang-ig-keit, wie

Adagio molto a tempo

To - des-angst mein Herz mit Macht er - greift! Ich lei-de sehr, _ mein _

Va - ter! o _ sieh! _ ich lei - de sehr, _ er - barm' dich mein!

Aria

68

Qua - len, von den Qua - len, die mir dräun. Schreck-en

71

fasst mich, und es zit - tert gräss - lich schau - dernd mein Ge -

cresc.

74

bein. Wie ein Fie - ber -

f *dim.* *p*

77

frost er - grei - fet mich die Angst, die

Mei-ne See - le ist er -

schüt - tert von den Qua - len, die mir dräun, von den

cresc.

Qua - len, die mir dräun, und von

f   *p*   *f*   *dim.*

mei - nem Ant - litz träu - fet, und von

p   *p*

Te ergo quæsumus

from

TE DEUM LAUDAMUS

Anton Bruckner

Moderato

Sanctus
from
ST. CECILIA MASS

Charles Gounod

Gentle airs, melodious strains!

from
ATHALIA

George Frideric Handel

*Small size notes are to be played only in the absence of a cello.

strains! _ call for rap - tures out of woe; _____ gen-tle airs, me-lo-dious

strains! _ call for rap - tures _ out of woe, _____ call for rap - tures out of

Adagio

Tempo I

woe.

ad libitum

mf

Gentle airs, melodious strains!

from
ATHALIA

George Frideric Handel

The part may be carefully cut from the book.

The enemy said

from

ISRAEL IN EGYPT

George Frideric Handel

The en-e-my said, I will pur-sue, I will o-ver-take, I will o-ver-

94

I will pur - sue, I'll o - ver - take, I will di - vide, I'll draw my sword; my hand shall _ de -

stroy _____ them, my hand, my hand shall _ de -

stroy __ them.

Waft her, angels

from

JEPHTHA

George Frideric Handel

Recit.

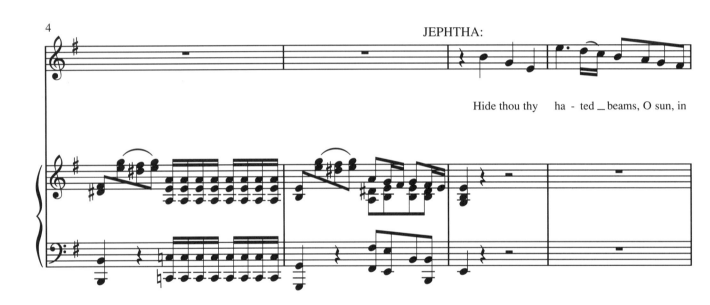

JEPHTHA:

Hide thou thy ha - ted ___ beams, O sun, in

clouds, in clouds and dark - ness, hide thou thy ha - ted

woe,   deep   as is a fa - ther's woe:

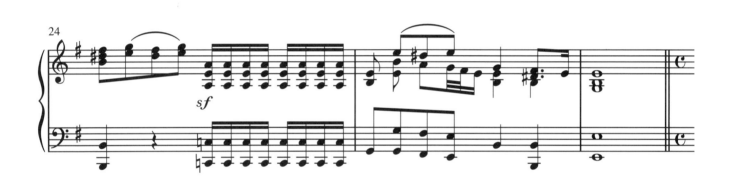

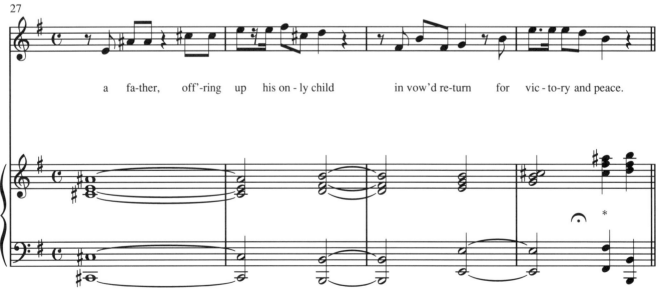

a fa-ther, off'-ring up   his on - ly child   in vow'd re-turn   for   vic - to-ry and peace.

*Play after the word "peace."

Aria

[**Andante larghetto**]

Waft her, an - gels, through the skies,

there like you for ev -

- er reign. Waft her, an - gels, through the

skies, waft her, an - gels, through the

skies, far a - bove yon a - zure plain, for a - bove yon a - zure

plain;   an - gels,   waft ⸺ her ⸺ through ⸺ the ⸺

skies,   waft ⸺ her ⸺ through ⸺ the ⸺ skies,   far ⸺ a - bove ⸺ yon ⸺ a - zure ⸺

plain, ⸺⸺⸺⸺⸺   far a - bove   yon a - zure plain.

Sound an alarm!
from
JUDAS MACCABÆUS

George Frideric Handel

Aria

Comfort ye, my people;
Ev'ry valley shall be exalted

from
MESSIAH

George Frideric Handel

*appoggiatura possible
**These final chords are customarily delayed until 1 beat after the voice finishes.

Aria

the crook - ed __ straight, and the rough plac - es

plain, __ the crook - ed

straight, the crook - ed straight, __ and rough plac - es plain, __

simile

Behold, and see if there be any sorrow;
But Thou didst not leave His soul in hell

from
MESSIAH

George Frideric Handel

an - y   to   com - fort him;   He   look - ed for some   to have pit - y   on Him,

but there was   no man,   nei - ther found He   an - y   to   com - fort Him.

Arioso

Largo e piano

Be - hold,   and _ see,   be - hold,   and   see   if

[*p*]

124

*appoggiatura optional

Recit.

He was cut off out of the land of the liv - ing:

for the trans - gres - sion of Thy peo - ple was He strick - en.

Aria

Andante larghetto

But Thou didst not leave His

soul in ___ hell, but Thou didst _ not _ leave His

soul in ___ hell, nor didst ___ Thou suf - fer, nor didst Thou suf - fer Thy

Ho - ly ___ One to see cor - rup - tion.

But Thou didst not leave His

nor didst Thou suf - fer, nor didst Thou suf - fer Thy

Ho - ly __ One, Thy Ho - ly __ One to see cor - rup - tion.

Thou shalt break them
from
MESSIAH

George Frideric Handel

He that dwell-eth in heav-en shall laugh them to scorn; the Lord shall have them in de-ri-sion.

Thou shalt break them, thou shalt

*The final 2 chords usually are played after the finish of the vocal line.

ter's ves - sel.

Thou shalt break them,

thou shalt break — them with a rod

of i - ron, thou shalt

Total eclipse
from
SAMSON

George Frideric Handel

Recit.

SAMSON:

Oh, loss of sight! of thee I most com - plain! Oh, worse than beg-gar-y, old

age, or chains! my ver - y soul in re - al dark-ness dwells.

Aria
[Larghetto]

To - tal e - clipse! no sun, no moon, All

*The final 2 chords are usually played after the finish of the vocal line.

Hier steht der Wand'rer nun
(The trav'ler stands perplexed)
from
DIE JAHRESZEITEN
(The Seasons)

Franz Joseph Haydn

65

und Mü - dig - keit und Frost ihm al - le
And wea - ri - ness and cold Have stiff - en'd

pp *simile*

72

Glie - der lähmt. Jetzt sin - ket ihm der Mut, und
all _____ his limbs. De - press'd his cou - rage sinks, And

simile

80

Angst be - klemmt sein Herz: doch plötz - lich trifft sein spä - hend Aug'
an - guish wrings his heart! Be - fore his glad - den'd sight ap - pears

f *p*

87

der Schim - mer ei - nes na - hen Lichts.
A sud - den gleam of neigh - b'ring light;

p

Mit Würd' und Hoheit angetan

(In native worth)

from

DIE SCHÖPFUNG

(The Creation)

Franz Joseph Haydn

Aria

Andante (♩ = 88)

Würd' und Ho - heit an - ge - tan, mit Schön - heit, Stärk' und _ Mut be - gabt, gen
na - tive worth and ho - nour clad, With beau - ty, cou - rage, _ strength, a-dorn'd, E -

47

Geist, des Schöp - fers Hauch und _ E - ben-
soul, *the* *breath* *and* *i* - *mage* _ *of* ___ *his*

pp

51

bild.
God.

f *fz* *simile* *f*

54

An sei - nen Bu - sen schmie - get sich, für
With *fond* - *ness* *leans* *up* - *on* *his breast* *The*

p

58

ihn, aus ihm ge - formt, die Gat - tin _ hold _ und _ an - muts-voll, die _ Gat - tin hold _ und _
part - *ner* *for* *him* _ *form'd,* *A* *wo* - *man,* _ *fair* _ *and* _ *grace* - *ful spouse, A* ___ *wom-an, fair* _ *and* _

Fac me cruce custodiri

from
STABAT MATER

Franz Joseph Haydn

cus-to - di - ri, mor - te præ-mu - ni - ri, con-ser - va - ri, gra - - - - - - - ti - a,

gra - ti - a.

If with all your hearts
(So ihr mich von ganzen Herzen suchet)
from
ELIJAH

Felix Mendelssohn

slow to an-ger, and mer-ci-ful, and kind, and gra-cious, and re-pent-eth Him of the e-vil.
gnä-dig, barm-her-zig, ge - dul-dig und von gro-sser Gü - te, und reut ____ ihn bald der Stra-fe.

Aria

Andante con moto ♩ = 72

'If with all your hearts ye tru-ly seek Me,
'So ihr mich von gan - zen Her-zen su - chet,

ye shall ev - er sure-ly find Me.' Thus saith our God, 'If with
so will ich mich fin-den las - sen' spricht un - ser Gott. 'So ihr

all your hearts ye tru-ly seek Me, ye shall ev - er sure-ly find Me.'
mich von gan - zen Her-zen su - chet, so will ich mich fin-den las - sen'

Then shall the righteous shine forth

(Dann werden die Gerechten leuchten)

from

ELIJAH

Felix Mendelssohn

heav'n - ly Fa - ther's realm, as the sun,___ as the sun ___ in their
rech - ten, leuch - ten, wie die Son - ne, wie die Son - ne in

heav'n-ly Fa - ther's_ realm.
ih - res Va - ters_ Reich.

Joy on their head shall be for ev - er-
Won - ne und Freu - de wer - den sie er-

last - ing, joy on their head shall be for ev - er - last - ing, and all sor - row and mourn - ing shall
grei - fen. Won - ne und Freu - de wer - den sie er - grei - fen. A - ber Trau - ern, Trau - ern und

flee a - way, shall flee a - way for - ev - er.
Seuf - zen wird vor ih - nen flie - hen, vor ih - nen flie - hen.

Then, then shall the right - eous shine forth as the sun in their heav'n-ly
Dann wer - den die Ge-rech - ten leuch - ten, wie die Son - ne in ih - res

Fa - ther's realm, shine forth, shine in their heav'n - ly Fa - ther's
Va - ters Reich. Leuch - ten, leuch - ten in ih - res Va - ters

Strikke des Todes
(The Sorrows of Death)
from
LOBGESANG
(Hymn of Praise)

Felix Mendelssohn

41

To - des hat - ten uns um - fan - gen, und Angst der Höl - le
death had clos - ed all a - round me, and Hell's dark ter - rors

46

hat - te uns ge - trof - fen, wir wan - del - ten in Fin - ster - nis, wir
had got hold up - on me, with trou - ble and deep heav - i - ness, with

52

wan - del - ten in Fin - ster - nis. Er a - ber spricht: Wa - che auf!
trou - ble and deep heav - i - ness. But, said the Lord, Come, a - rise,

Sei getreu bis in den Tod
(Be thou faithful unto death)
from
PAULUS
(St. Paul)

Felix Mendelssohn

Gratias agimus tibi
from
MESSA DI GLORIA

Giacomo Puccini

Domine Deus
from
MESSE SOLENNELLE

Gioachino Rossini

Cujus animam

from

STABAT MATER

Gioachino Rossini

a - ni - mam ge - men - tem, __ con - tris -

tan - tem __ et do - len - tem, per - tran -

si - vit __ gla - di - us.

Cu - jus __ a - ni - mam ge - men - tem, __

simile

194

na - ti pœ - - - nas in - cly - ti.

Domine, ego credidi

from
ORATORIO DE NOËL
(Christmas Oratorio)

Camille Saint-Saëns

Ingemisco
from
MESSA DI REQUIEM

Giuseppe Verdi

ques - tra, In - ter o - ves lo - cum

præ - sta, Et ab hæ - dis me se - que -

stra, Sta - tu - ens, Sta - tu -

Peccator videbit

from
BEATUS VIR

Antonio Vivaldi

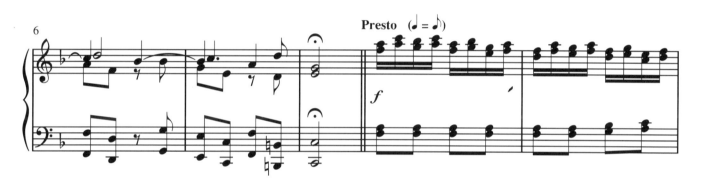

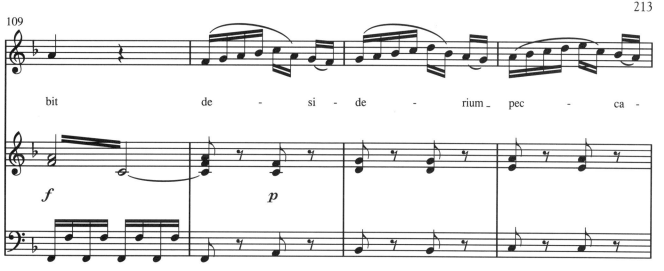

bit   de - si - de - rium pec - ca -

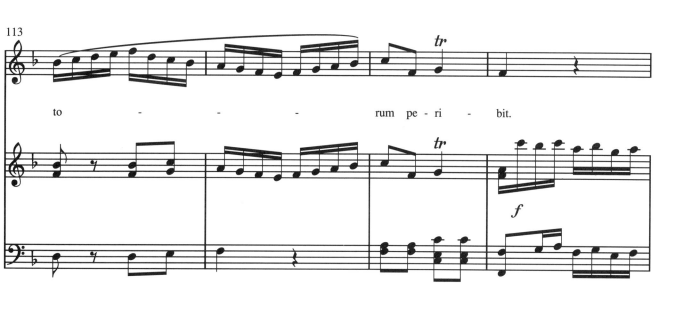

to - - - rum pe - ri - bit.